Microwave Dessert Cookbook for Busy People

34 Microwave Recipes That Are So Easy and Simple

BY: Allie Allen

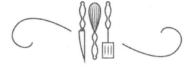

COOK & ENJOY

Copyright 2019 Allie Allen

Copyright Notes

This book is written as an informational tool. While the author has taken every precaution to ensure the accuracy of the information provided therein, the reader is warned that they assume all risk when following the content. The author will not be held responsible for any damages that may occur as a result of the readers' actions.

The author does not give permission to reproduce this book in any form, including but not limited to: print, social media posts, electronic copies or photocopies, unless permission is expressly given in writing.

Contents

Delicious Microwave Dessert Recipes

ssssssssssssssssssssssssssssssssssssssssssssssssssss

1) Microwaved Choco Muffins

This is a five-minute microwave dessert and/or breakfast muffin that you can easily whip up, even without baking experience.

List of Ingredients:

- 2 tablespoons cocoa powder
- 4 tablespoons whole meal plain flour
- 3 tablespoons sunflower oil
- 2 tablespoons whisked egg
- 1/3 teaspoons baking powder
- 3 tbsps. milk
- 4 tbsps. demerara sugar
- 1 drop vanilla extract
- 2 teaspoons chocolate chips

sssssssssssssssssssssssssssssssssssssssssssssssssss

Procedure:

Gather all your ingredients and pour into a huge mug. Mix well to combine. Sprinkle with some sugar then pop the mug into the microwave and cook for 3 minutes. The mixture should rise, and become bubbly. Remove from the microwave and let cool for a few minutes. Serve straight from the cup or turn it upside down on a plate. Add a dollop of yoghurt of nuts before serving.

2) Simple Cookies and Cream Mug Cake

This dessert is so tasty, sinful yet satisfying. It's easy to make too!

List of Ingredients:

- 2 pcs Oreos
- ¼ teaspoons baking powder
- 4 tablespoons milk
- ¼ cup white chocolate chips
- ¼ cup all-purpose flour

sssssssssssssssssssssssssssssssssssssssssssssssssssss

Procedure:

Inside a microwave-safe mug, put 3 tablespoons milk and white chocolate chips. Pop it inside the microwave for half a minute to allow the chocolates to melt. Take the mug out and stir slightly. Pop it back for 20 seconds to make the chocolate smooth.

When chocolate is smooth and quite thickened, stir in the baking powder and flour. Mix the ingredients with a whisk until a batter forms.

Add the remaining milk and combine thoroughly. Add in the Oreos and crumble with a fork. Place the mug into the microwave for 1 minute. Let the cake cool and set for 20 minutes before serving.

3) Easy Microwaved Apple Crisp

Indulge in this super simple dessert treat featuring apples and a slew of delicious ingredients.

List of Ingredients:

- 6 cups apples, peeled and wedged
- ½ cup brown sugar
- 1 teaspoon cinnamon
- ½ cup rolled oats
- ¼ teaspoons salt
- ¼ cup butter
- ¾ cup all-purpose flour
- Whipped cream or ice cream to top

ssssssssssssssssssssssssssssssssssssssssssssssssss

Procedure:

Place the apples in microwave-safe dish that has been lightly sprayed with oil. Meanwhile, combine flour, oats, salt, cinnamon and sugar in another container. Mix thoroughly. Use a pastry blender to cut butter and top into the apples. Sprinkle the combined dry ingredients into the apples and toss lightly. Microwave the apples for 15 minutes. Let cool and top with whipped cream or ice cream before serving.

4) Chocolate Fudge S'mores

Fudgy, chocolate-y and just so sinfully good, this chocolate fudge s'mores are forever a classic. The best thing is, you can whip it up yourself in just in just 5 minutes!

List of Ingredients:

- ¼ cup whole wheat pastry flour
- 3 tbsps. graham cracker crumbs
- 1/8 teaspoons baking powder
- 2 tbsps. unsweetened dark cocoa powder
- 1 large egg
- ½ teaspoons vanilla extract
- 3 ½ tbsps. melted unsalted butter
- 1 ½ ounces chopped milk chocolate
- 2 tbsps. granulated sugar
- Pinch of salt
- Marshmallows

sssssssssssssssssssssssssssssssssssssssssssssssssssss

Procedure:

In small bowl, mix an ounce of chocolate with 2 tbsps. of melted butter. Pop into the microwave and heat for 30 seconds. Meanwhile, combine 2 tbsps. graham crumbs with the remaining butter. Mix well until graham becomes a little moist. Press this mixture at the bottom of your mug or cup.

In a slightly larger bowl, combine vanilla, egg and sugar. Add in the baking powder, cocoa, salt and flour until you are able to form a batter. Add the melted butter and chocolate you have previously prepared into the flour mixture. Stir in the remaining chocolates and fold it into the mixture, followed by 1 tablespoon of graham crumbs and a few marshmallows. Put the mug into the microwave 1:30-2 minutes. Take out the mug, put a few marshmallows on top and microwave again for 5 seconds. Serve and enjoy.

5) Homemade Baileys Fudge

This fudge will rekindle the youth in you yet make you feel all-grown up. How is that? Give this Baileys Fudge a shot.

List of Ingredients:

- 1 can condensed milk
- 1 ½ teaspoons vanilla extract
- 1 tablespoon butter
- 250g caster sugar
- 2 tablespoons Baileys
- 250g soft brown sugar

sssssssssssssssssssssssssssssssssssssssssssssssss

Procedure:

Combine the sugars, butter and condensed milk in large bowl. Whisk until they are properly incorporated. Microwave the mixture for 9 minutes (for a 900W microwave). Take it out every 3 minutes to stir. Once the mixture is cooked, add in the Baileys and vanilla extract and whisk until it looks smooth. Pour into a lined tin and let cool. You can also refrigerate so it sets better.

6) Easy Strawberry Shortcake

Reminiscent of full-fledged strawberry shortcake, this mug microwave version is easier to produce and perfect for random sweet cravings.

List of Ingredients:

- 3 tablespoons self-rising flour
- 1 tablespoon sugar
- 1 tablespoon cold butter, cut into tiny pieces
- ½ cup whipped cream
- 1 tablespoon heavy cream
- 1/8 teaspoons salt
- 7 strawberries, sliced

sssssssssssssssssssssssssssssssssssssssssssssssssssss

Procedure:

Place the butter and sugar into the bottom of mug. Mash them together with a fork until thoroughly combined. Mix until the mixture becomes slightly crumbly. Add salt and flour and mix thoroughly. Pour the heavy cream and fold. Pop the mug into the microwave for 45-seconds to 1 minute. Poke the middle with a toothpick and see if the mixture still clings. Microwave again for another 20 minutes and check with a toothpick again. If it comes out clean, put the whipped cream on top of the mug followed by a garnishing of sliced strawberries.

7) Red Velvet Cookie

Enjoy your very own homemade red velvet cookie at home that's warm, fresh off the microwave and utterly delicious.

List of Ingredients:

- 2 tablespoons red velvet cake mix
- 1 tablespoon butter
- ¼ teaspoons vanilla extract
- 2 tablespoons flour
- 1 tablespoon granulated white sugar
- 1 egg yolk
- 1 tablespoon dark brown sugar
- A pinch of salt

sssssssssssssssssssssssssssssssssssssssssssssssssssss

Procedure:

Place butter in a mug and microwave until melted. Stir in salt, sugar and vanilla. Mix thoroughly. Add in the egg yolk and whisk. Add red velvet mix and flour and stir. Microwave the mug for 1 minute and let cool before serving.

8) Banana Cake in a Mug

This sweet treat is perfect for dessert but you can have it any time of day! This is also healthier than store-bought ones because you can control the amount of sugar and flour. And oh, it has coffee too so it's a great pick-me-upper.

List of Ingredients:

- 1 ripe mashed banana
- ½ teaspoons baking powder
- 1 tablespoon melted butter
- 1 tablespoon milk
- 3 tablespoons brown sugar
- 1 egg, slightly beaten
- 3 tablespoons plain flour
- 1 scoop coffee ice cream

ssssssssssssssssssssssssssssssssssssssssssssssssssss

Procedure:

Place butter into a microwave-safe mug for 10 seconds to melt. Stir in milk and egg, combining them with butter using a fork. Combine mashed banana into mixture and mix well. Add all the dry ingredients and mix thoroughly. Microwave the mug for a minute. The mixture should rise and resemble a pudding. The center should become gooey but if this is not achieved in one minute, pop the mug back into the microwave for 10-second bursts until it is gooey enough to your liking. Add a scoop of coffee ice cream on top and serve right away.

9) Easy Mug Pancake

This is a different and special way to enjoy pancakes and far easier to create in the morning for breakfast or as midnight snack.

List of Ingredients:

- 2 tablespoons gluten-free all-purpose flour mix
- 3 tablespoons butter
- 1 large egg
- 3 tablespoons milk
- 2 tablespoons oat flour
- 3 tablespoons maple syrup
- ¼ teaspoons baking soda

ssssssssssssssssssssssssssssssssssssssssssssssssssss

Procedure:

Place butter into the mug and melt in the microwave for 3 minutes. Take out the mug and let cool. Add the dry ingredients into the butter and whisk. Add in egg, milk and maple syrup. Mix well to combine. Put the mug in the microwave for 3 minutes. Once the microwave is turned off, let it stay there for 2 more minutes. Drizzle with maple syrup before serving.

10) Quick and Easy Carrot Cake Mug

Put those extra carrots to use and create a few mugs of these carrot cakes that the whole family will enjoy.

List of Ingredients:

- 1 carrot, grated
- ½ teaspoons baking powder
- ¼ cup flour
- 1 tablespoon milk
- ½ teaspoons vanilla
- ½ teaspoons cinnamon
- 1 tablespoon coconut oil
- 1 tablespoon sugar
- ¼ teaspoons nutmeg
- Dash of salt

sssssssssssssssssssssssssssssssssssssssssssssssssssss

Procedure:

Get a mug and put the flour, sugar, cinnamon, nutmeg, salt, sugar and baking powder. Stir thoroughly to combine. Add the vanilla, milk and coconut oil. Combine with the other ingredients. Stir in the grated carrot and mix. Place the mug in the microwave for 90 seconds, checking on the first minute. For more flavor, adding vanilla yogurt is optional.

11) Russian Fudge

Here's a different type of fudge: it is chocolate-less and it is no-fuss. Just microwave it and it's yours in just 15 minutes!

List of Ingredients:

- 200g condensed milk
- ½ cup skim milk
- 1 tablespoon golden syrup
- 125g chopped butter, room temperature
- 2 ½ cups caster sugar
- 1 teaspoon vanilla
- A pinch of salt

sssssssssssssssssssssssssssssssssssssssssssssssssssssss

Procedure:

Combine all ingredients in a microwave-safe bowl and mix. Microwave the mixture for 15 minutes, checking in every 3 minutes to mix the ingredients with a spoon to make sure they are thoroughly incorporated as they cook. Transfer the fudge into a lined tin or baking dish with waxed paper. Let cool. Slice and serve.

12) Easiest Mug Brownie

Got a brownie craving? No need to hit the stores. This mug recipe is easily done within 5-minutes, perfect for last-minute notice for entertaining or midnight snacking.

List of Ingredients:

- 2 tablespoons natural unsweetened cocoa
- ¼ cup water
- ¼ cup flour
- 2 drops vanilla extract
- 2 tablespoons heavy whipped cream
- 2 tablespoons vegetable oil
- A dash of salt
- A dash of cinnamon

sssssssssssssssssssssssssssssssssssssssssssssssssssss

Procedure:

Combine flour, salt, cocoa and cinnamon in a microwave-safe mug until clumps are broken down. Add vanilla, water and vegetable oil. Mix thoroughly until lumps have disappeared and the mixture becomes smooth. Pop into the microwave for 2 minutes, checking every minute to make sure that it does not become too dry. The brownie should still be smooth when you take it out. Add 2 tablespoons of heavy whipped cream before serving.

13) Microwave Sponge Pudding

Here's a delicious pudding with some very basic ingredients and simple procedure, all done within 15 minutes!

List of Ingredients:

- 2 oz. self-rising flour
- 2 oz. butter
- 2 tablespoons milk
- 2 oz. caster sugar
- 1 egg, lightly beaten
- 2 tablespoons of fruit jam of choice

sssssssssssssssssssssssssssssssssssssssssssssssssss

Procedure:

Combine butter and sugar in a small bowl. Whisk until creamy and smooth. Add in the milk slowly and steadily while whisking. Sift flour on top and gently fold with the mixture. Take a microwave-safe mug and place a few spoons of fruit jam of choice. Pour over the batter. Microwave for 3-4 minutes until the pudding is set. Serve while hot.

14) Single Serving Cinnamon Bun Cake in a Mug

For when you want a piece (or mug) of cake, and eat it too, here's an easy way to do so.

List of Ingredients:

- 2 tablespoons applesauce
- ¼ cup flour
- 1 tablespoon buttermilk
- 1 tablespoon vegetable oil
- 2 ½ tablespoons light brown sugar
- ¼ teaspoons vanilla extract
- ¼ teaspoons baking powder
- 1/8 teaspoons salt
- ¾ teaspoons ground cinnamon
- Dash of nutmeg

sssssssssssssssssssssssssssssssssssssssssssssssssssssss

Procedure:

Place all the ingredients into a mug and combine thoroughly. Put the mug into the oven for 1 minute. Serve and enjoy.

15) Blueberry Flax Muffin

Want a muffin for dessert? What about for breakfast? This is the one you need. Much healthier than the store-bought ones, making them is fun too!

List of Ingredients:

- 1 oz. blueberries, fresh or frozen
- ½ teaspoons orange zest
- ¼ cup ground flaxseed
- ½ teaspoons nutmeg
- 2 tablespoons sugar-free pancake syrup
- ½ teaspoons baking powder
- 1 egg white

sssssssssssssssssssssssssssssssssssssssssssssssssssssss

Procedure:

Mix blueberries, orange zest, flaxseed, nutmeg and baking powder inside a mug. Combine thoroughly. Pour in the egg white and syrup then whisk. Pop the mug into the microwave for 1 minute and 30 seconds. If desired, top with more syrup or butter before serving.

16) Microwave Apple Cinnamon Cake

This is a very filling sweet treat that you can make that's a bit spongy, creamy and delicious all in one serving!

List of Ingredients:

For the Cake

- 1 heaping tablespoon brown sugar
- ½ tablespoons vegetable oil
- 1 tablespoon applesauce
- ½ tablespoons milk
- 3 tablespoons flour
- 1/8 teaspoons baking powder
- 1/8 teaspoons vanilla extract
- ½ teaspoons ground cinnamon

For the Icing

- 1 teaspoon milk
- 1 tablespoon cream cheese in room temperature
- 2 tablespoons powdered sugar

SS

Procedure:

Begin with the icing by combining milk, cream cheese powdered sugar. Mix thoroughly and set aside.

For the cake, just mix all the dry ingredients inside a microwave-safe bowl or ramekin. Add the applesauce, milk, vanilla and vegetable oil. Be careful not to over-mix the ingredients. On high setting, microwave the mixture for 45 seconds to 1 minute. Garnish with icing and serve.

17) Chocolate Cake Muffin

Here's a good way to indulge your sweet tooth yet making sure you're not overloading with sugar. This recipe has been properly portioned to give you the best of both worlds

List of Ingredients:

<u>For the cake muffin:</u>

- 3 tablespoons whole wheat flour
- 15 drops Stevia
- 1 egg white
- ½ teaspoons baking powder
- 1 tablespoon unsweetened cocoa powder
- 2 tablespoons unsweetened almond milk
- 1 teaspoon organic sugar
- Dark chocolate chips for garnishing

<u>For the peanut butter sauce:</u>

- 1 teaspoon unsweetened cocoa powder
- 1 teaspoon peanut butter

ssssssssssssssssssssssssssssssssssssssssssssssssssssss

Procedure:

Gather the ingredients for the cake muffin and combine in a microwave-safe mug. Mix thoroughly. Microwave for 1 minute and 30 seconds. Meanwhile, prepare the sauce by heating the peanut butter until melted in a microwave for 20 seconds. Stir in unsweetened cocoa powder and mix. Pour the sauce mixture into the cake muffin. Sprinkle with a few dark chocolate chips. Serve and enjoy.

18) Nutella Cake

Want a twist to your favorite Nutella? Turn it into a cake. Here's a very easy way to do it.

List of Ingredients:

- 4 tablespoons self-rising flour
- 3 tbsps. Nutella
- 3 tbsps. vegetable oil
- 4 tbsps. sugar
- 3 tablespoons milk
- 3 tablespoons cocoa powder
- 1 egg

ssssssssssssssssssssssssssssssssssssssssssssssssssssssss

Procedure:

In a microwave-safe cup or mug, place all the ingredients and combine thoroughly. Bake in the microwave for 1 – 3 minutes, checking every minute to make sure it doesn't get too dry. The time duration will depend on the power of your microwave.

19) Molten Caramel Mug Cake

Sweet gooey caramel mug cake beats even the worst of moods and makes a perfect and thoughtful gesture for the one you love.

List of Ingredients:

- 1 teaspoon brown sugar
- 2 tablespoons caramel sauce
- 1/8 teaspoons baking soda
- 1/8 teaspoons baking powder
- 2 tablespoons all-purpose flour
- 2 teaspoons vegetable oil
- 2 teaspoons milk
- A pinch of salt
- Funfetti

ssssssssssssssssssssssssssssssssssssssssssssssssssss

Procedure:

Take a small bowl and combine brown sugar, baking powder, salt, baking soda and flour. Stir in milk, oil and a tablespoon of caramel sauce. Combine the ingredients until it forms into a batter. Be careful not to over mix or else the mixture will turn out too tough. Transfer half of the batter into a microwave-safe mug. Pour some funfetti into the center then cover with the remaining batter. Microwave the mixture for 1 minute and 30 seconds. Let cool for a few minutes. Sprinkle more funfetti and a tablespoon of caramel sauce before serving.

20) Homemade Lemon Bars

Here's a zesty treat to end your meal: a dessert with deliciously tender crust filled with an equally unforgettable lemon filling.

List of Ingredients:

For the Crust:

- 6 tablespoons melted butter
- 1 cup flour
- 3 tablespoons powdered sugar
- 1 tablespoon lemon zest

For the Filling:

- 1 cup sugar
- 1 tablespoon flour
- 3 eggs
- ½ teaspoons baking powder
- 2 tablespoons lemon zest
- 1/3 cup lemon juice
- ¼ teaspoons salt

sss

Procedure:

For the crust, put together powdered sugar and flour. Stir in the lemon zest and combine them thoroughly. Add the melted butter. Knead the flour mixture into dough. Put the dough into a baking pan and press into a crust. Bake the dough in the microwave for 3 minutes.

For the filling, mix eggs, lemon juice, sugar and lemon zest in a bowl. Mix them together with a whisk then add in the salt, flour and baking powder. Pour the filling mixture over the crust and microwave for 3-4 minutes or until the filling has set.

21) Chocolate Protein Mug Cake

Here's a great way to make your dessert be energy-giving: add protein into it. This is an excellent dessert if you're quite the health buff or just wants to have some protein and sugar high on a lazy day.

List of Ingredients:

- 1 tablespoon chocolate protein powder
- 1 teaspoon coconut oil
- 1/8 teaspoons baking powder
- 4 tablespoons unsweetened almond milk
- 1 tablespoon coconut palm sugar
- 2 tablespoons whole-wheat flour
- 1 large egg, lightly beaten

sssssssssssssssssssssssssssssssssssssssssssssssssss

Procedure:

Place all the dry ingredients into a bowl and combine thoroughly. Add in the wet ingredients and mix. Spray or brush a microwave-safe mug with oil, then transfer the batter. Microwave for 1 minute on high. Let cool slightly and serve.

22) Apple Crumble

This is a fun way to keep your orchard apples from rotting. Tangy and low in sugar, this dessert is fun to make and healthy to eat.

List of Ingredients:

<u>For the Apples:</u>

- 1 tablespoon unsweetened almond milk
- 2 apples
- 1 teaspoon vanilla
- 1 teaspoon cinnamon
- A few drops of lemon juice

<u>For the Crumble:</u>

- 1 tablespoon butter
- 1 cup rolled oats
- 1 tablespoon coconut palm sugar
- 1 tablespoon coconut oil
- ½ cup Greek yoghurt
- A dash of cinnamon

SS

Procedure:

Peel the apples and slice into small pieces. Put them into a medium-sized bowl and stir in almond milk, vanilla cinnamon and lemon juice. Mix well. Divide the apple mixture into four mugs and set aside.

For the crumble, mix all the ingredients, excluding the Greek yoghurt, in a bowl. Use your hands to make the mixture a little clumpy. Top into the mugs filled with the apple mixture and microwave for 6-8 minutes until the apples have reached your desired softness. Top each mug with yoghurt and a dash of cinnamon before serving.

23) Oatmeal Nutella Mug Cake

With just the right hint of nutty, gooey and decadence, you don't have to be an experienced baker to come up with this divine mug cake.

List of Ingredients:

- 1 ½ tablespoons rolled oats
- 3 tablespoons milk
- 1 tablespoon Nutella
- 1/8 teaspoon salt
- 1 tablespoon sugar
- 1 tablespoon finely chopped pecans,
- 1 tablespoon coconut oil
- ¼ teaspoon cinnamon
- 3 tablespoons flour
- ¼ teaspoon baking powder
- Pinch of nutmeg

sssssssssssssssssssssssssssssssssssssssssssssssssssss

Procedure:

In huge mug, combine oil, milk and sugar. Mix well. Add the flour and whisk until the mixture becomes smooth. Stir in pecans and oats; salt, baking powder, nutmeg and cinnamon. Mix thoroughly.

Take a spoonful of Nutella and drop into the middle of the batter. Microwave the mixture for one minute, followed by 30-seconds bursts, constantly checking that top is dry but not overly so. Let cool slightly. Serve and enjoy.

24) Homemade Vanilla Bean Mug Cake

Rich, creamy and extremely easy to make, this vanilla bean mug cake you can create and recreate any time of the day or when your sweet tooth bugs you.

List of Ingredients:

<u>Ingredients for the Cake</u>

- ¼ teaspoons baking powder
- ½ teaspoons vanilla bean paste
- 3 tablespoons all-purpose flour
- 1 tablespoon melted butter
- 3 tablespoons skim milk
- 1.5 tablespoons sugar
- Salt to taste

<u>Ingredients for the Frosting</u>

- ¼ teaspoons vanilla bean paste
- 1 ½ tablespoons cream cheese in room temperature
- 2 tablespoons powdered sugar

SSS

Procedure:

For the cake, simply mix all the dry ingredients for the cake thoroughly inside a ramekin or a mug. Add the milk, butter and vanilla paste. Combine them well. Microwave the mixture for 1 minute. Take it out of the microwave and set aside.

Gather the ingredients for the frosting, mix well and top directly onto the cake. Serve and enjoy.

25) Avocado Mug Cake

This recipe provides a tropical punch to your ordinary cake. It's fun and easy to do too!

List of Ingredients:

- Half of avocado, mashed
- ¼ teaspoons baking powder
- 5 tablespoons non-fat milk
- 4 tablespoons flour
- 4 ½ tablespoons sugar

sssssssssssssssssssssssssssssssssssssssssssssssssssss

Procedure:

Combine the ingredients inside a mug and mix until mixture becomes smooth. Microwave for 2 minutes. Pierce a toothpick into the center of the mug. If it comes out clean, it's good to serve.

26) Eggless Chocolate Chip Cookie

Chocolate chip cookies just seem to rekindle the kids in us. Here's an eggless recipe to try with your microwave today.

List of Ingredients:

- 2 tablespoons semi-sweet chocolate chips
- 2 teaspoons whole milk
- 2 tablespoons light brown sugar
- 1 tablespoon melted unsalted butter
- 3 tablespoons all-purpose flour
- 1/8 teaspoons vanilla extract
- Peanut butter
- A dash of salt

sssssssssssssssssssssssssssssssssssssssssssssssssss

Procedure:

Combine light brown sugar and melted butter in small bowl. Whisk in salt, milk and vanilla extract. Mix thoroughly. Add in the flour and fold. Stir in semi-sweet chocolate chip cookies until the mixture is thoroughly combined. Transfer into a microwave dish and bake at 700W for 30 seconds. Microwave again at 700W but this time in 20 seconds. Finally, repeat the process in 10 seconds. Cookie should be done when the center is set. Take it out of the microwave and spread some peanut butter on top before serving.

27) Flourless Chocolate Mug Cake

This is chocolate cake made very easy! Take out flour from the equation and you have a decadent chocolate cake straight from the microwave.

List of Ingredients:

- 1 ½ teaspoons cocoa powder
- ½ cup chocolate chips
- 2 tablespoons granulated sugar
- 2 tablespoons unsalted butter
- 1 egg, lightly beaten
- 1 teaspoon salt
- ½ teaspoons
- ½ teaspoons vanilla extract
- A sprinkling of confectioner's sugar
- Some fresh berries for garnishing

sssssssssssssssssssssssssssssssssssssssssssssssssss

Procedure:

Deduct 2 tablespoons of chocolate chips and pour the remaining into a microwave-safe bowl. Heat the chocolate chips in the microwave for 20-seconds bursts until melted. Pour the vanilla into the melted chocolate and stir in the butter. Mix thoroughly until smooth. Set aside to cool.

In another bowl, mix lightly beaten egg with sugar. Stir in salt and continue mixing until it thickens. Add the chocolate mixture and fold. Stir in 2 tablespoons chocolate chips and mix. Sift cocoa powder and combine into the mixture.

Transfer the mixture into microwave-safe mugs and bake for 2 minutes. Pierce the mug with a toothpick to check if the center is gooey as desired. Take the mugs out, sprinkle the top with confectioner's sugar and garnish with fresh berries.

28) Salted Caramel Cake

With just the right mix of sweet and salty, this deliciously decadent mug cake deserves another batch.

List of Ingredients:

- 2 salted caramels
- 3 tablespoons unsweetened cocoa powder
- 4 tablespoons all-purpose flour
- 1 tablespoon vegetable oil
- 4 tablespoons sugar
- 1 egg, lightly beaten
- 3 tablespoons skim milk
- ¼ teaspoons salt
- ¼ teaspoons baking powder

sssssssssssssssssssssssssssssssssssssssssssssssssssss

Procedure:

Take a small bowl and combine cocoa, egg, skim milk, vegetable oil, baking powder, flour, sugar and salt. Mix thoroughly. Transfer the mixture into a microwave-safe mug and put the salted caramel in the center. Microwave the mug for 1 min 30 sec. If you like it less gooey, add 30 seconds more in the microwave.

29) Chocolate Lava Cake in a Mug

This is an exquisite easy-to-do-dessert that you can complete within a few minutes using very simple ingredients.

List of Ingredients:

- 2 tablespoons unsweetened cocoa powder
- 1 tablespoon Nutella
- ¼ cup flour
- 2 tablespoons granulated sugar
- ¼ teaspoons baking powder
- 2 tablespoons vegetable oil
- ¼ cup milk
- A pinch of salt
- A scoop of vanilla ice cream to serve

sssssssssssssssssssssssssssssssssssssssssssssssssss

Procedure:

In a medium-sized bowl, combine baking powder, flour, granulated sugar, salt and cocoa powder. Mix thoroughly then add the vegetable oil and milk. Pour the batter into a microwave-safe mug, then drop a spoonful of Nutella into the middle. Pop the mug into the microwave for 70 seconds in high setting. Top it off with a scoop of vanilla ice cream and serve.

30) Peanut Butter Swirl Brownie

Chocolate and peanut butter is the perfect combo, but mix them together into a brownie recipe? Even better!

List of Ingredients:

- 1 tablespoon cocoa powder
- 2 tablespoons sugar
- 1 egg yolk
- 3 tablespoons flour
- 2 tablespoons softened butter
- Pinch of salt
- Splash of vanilla
- 1 tablespoon slightly warmed peanut butter
- 1 ½ Tablespoons brown sugar

ssssssssssssssssssssssssssssssssssssssssssssssssss

Procedure:

Combine the egg yolk, sugar, butter and brown sugar inside a ramekin. Mix thoroughly. Stir in flour and salt and mix again. You can add some chocolate chip cookies at this point if desired. Pour a tablespoon of warmed peanut butter and lightly swirl it using the tip of a toothpick. Pop the ramekin into the microwave for 1 minute and 30 seconds. Serve and enjoy.

31) Microwave Bread Pudding

This microwave dessert is so filling that it can double as your breakfast if served warm.

List of Ingredients:

- 4 cups sliced bread, cubed
- 2 cups skim milk
- ½ cup brown sugar
- 2 teaspoons vanilla
- ½ cup raisins
- 1 teaspoon margarine
- 2 eggs, lightly beaten
- A dash of cinnamon

ssssssssssssssssssssssssssssssssssssssssssssssssssss

Procedure:

In a microwave-safe casserole dish, place the bread. Add the raisins, cinnamon and brown sugar. Set aside. Meanwhile, in a small microwave-safe bowl, combine margarine, vanilla and milk and microwave this for 4 minutes. Stir in rapidly the beaten eggs into the milk mixture and pour into the bread in the casserole. Microwave the casserole for 10-12 minutes. Serve whether hot or cold, depending on what you prefer.

32) Chocolate Espresso Mug Cake

Soft, divine and utterly inviting, this is a very versatile cake mug that can fit different moods and seasons.

List of Ingredients:

- 2 tablespoons sweetened cocoa powder
- ¼ teaspoons baking powder
- 3 tablespoons all-purpose flour
- 1 egg
- ½ teaspoons vanilla extract
- 2 tablespoons milk
- 1 teaspoon instant coffee powder
- 3 tablespoons sugar
- 2 tablespoons oil

sssssssssssssssssssssssssssssssssssssssssssssssssssss

Procedure:

Combine flour, sugar, baking powder and coffee powder in a small bowl. Mix well. Add in the oil, milk, milk and egg until fully combined. Transfer the mixture in a mug and microwave for 90 seconds. Optional: top with a scoop of vanilla ice cream or a sprinkling of powdered sugar.

33) Scalloped Apples in a Mug

Enjoy this treat slightly with the apples tender to your liking and slightly warm and you have a comfort food slash dessert made oh-so-easy!

List of Ingredients:

- 8 medium-sized apples, peeled and sliced into bite-size pieces
- ½ teaspoons Cinnamon
- 2 tablespoons cubed butter
- 1/3 cup sugar
- ¼ teaspoons ground nutmeg
- 2 tablespoons cornstarch

sssssssssssssssssssssssssssssssssssssssssssssssssssss

Procedure:

Place the sliced apples into a microwave safe bowl. In a separate bowl, mix cinnamon, sugar, cornstarch and nutmeg. Pour this into the apples and toss to cover. Add cubes of butter on top of the tossed apples. Cover the bowl with aluminum foil and microwave for 15 minutes, stirring every 5 minutes. The apples are done when they are tender to your liking.

34) Pumpkin Oatmeal Cookie
in a Mug

Are you a vegan or would just want to add a dose of fiber into your meals? Here's a dessert to answer that. Chewy, filling delicious, this is a good way to enjoy your dessert guilt-free.

List of Ingredients:

- 2 tablespoons pumpkin (canned is optional)
- ¼ cup applesauce
- 3 tablespoons rolled oats
- ½ teaspoons pumpkin pie spice
- 2 teaspoons ground flaxseed
- 3 tablespoons almond milk
- 1 tablespoon peanut butter
- ¼ teaspoons cinnamon
- 3 teaspoons raisins

sssssssssssssssssssssssssssssssssssssssssssssssssssssss

Procedure:

Grease a microwave-safe baking dish or bowl and combine all ingredients thoroughly inside. Microwave for 4-6 minutes. Set aside to cool, serve and enjoy.

About the Author

Allie Allen developed her passion for the culinary arts at the tender age of five when she would help her mother cook for their large family of 8. Even back then, her family knew this would be more than a hobby for the young Allie and when she graduated from high school, she applied to cooking school in London. It had always been a dream of the young chef to study with some of Europe's best and she made it happen by attending the Chef Academy of London.

After graduation, Allie decided to bring her skills back to North America and open up her own restaurant. After 10 successful years as head chef and owner, she decided to sell her business and pursue other career avenues. This monumental decision led Allie to her true calling, teaching. She also started to write e-books for her students to study at home for practice. She is now the proud author of several e-books and gives private and semi-private cooking lessons to a range of students at all levels of experience.

Stay tuned for more from this dynamic chef and teacher when she releases more informative e-books on cooking and baking in the near future. Her work is infused with stores and anecdotes you will love!

Author's Afterthoughts

I can't tell you how grateful I am that you decided to read my book. My most heartfelt thanks that you took time out of your life to choose my work and I hope you find benefit within these pages.

There are so many books available today that offer similar content so that makes it even more humbling that you decided to buying mine.

Tell me what you thought! I am eager to hear your opinion and ideas on what you read as are others who are looking for a good book to buy. Leave a review on Amazon.com so others can benefit from your wisdom!

With much thanks,

Allie Allen

Made in the USA
Las Vegas, NV
27 May 2022

49444364R00042